This book belongs to:

_____

The Signing Kids Present
LEARNING SIGN LANGUAGE THROUGH LAUGHTER

Written and Created by Debra J. Visneuski Fontaine   Illustrated by Carlo Lo Raso

The Signing Kids Present
Learning Sign Language Through Laughter
Copyright © 2021 Debra J. Visneuski Fontaine

Produced and printed by Stillwater River Publications.
All rights reserved. Written and produced in the United States of America.
This book may not be reproduced or sold in any form without the expressed,
written permission of the author and publisher.

Visit our website at
www.StillwaterPress.com
for more information.

First Stillwater River Publications Edition

ISBN: 978-1-955123-69-3

Library of Congress Control Number: 2021925613

12345678910
Written by Debra J. Visneuski Fontaine
Illustrated by Carlo Lo Raso
Published by Stillwater River Publications,
Pawtucket, RI, USA.

*The views and opinions expressed
in this book are solely those of the author
and do not necessarily reflect the views
and opinions of the publisher.*

The Signing Kids Present

LEARNING SIGN LANGUAGE THROUGH LAUGHTER

This book is filled with signs and laughs,
from balancing bears to shopping giraffes.

You'll sign, "I see" to start each page,
each kid and adult, whatever your age!

The Signing Kids will show you how
to sign each word, like "boat" and "cow."

Each sentence is silly,
a fun way to sign.
You'll giggle and learn at the very
same time.

Every page has a letter, A to Z. And then
you'll have so much fun you'll start over
again.

Here we go!

On each page there is a sentence beginning with "I see." Please practice the signs for "I" and "See" a couple of times before moving on to the first sentence. Repeat signing "I see" at the beginning of each sentence, followed by the signed number of animals shown, and the sentence the Signing Kids will teach you.

I

- The sign for "I" is simply pointing to yourself with your index finger.

See

- Using either hand, extend your index and middle finger together creating a "V" shape.
- Place your hand in front of either eye, as shown, and bring your hand forward indicating that you see what's around you with your eyes.

I see 2

Alligators

- Separate all fingers on both hands.
- Place right hand (down-turned) on top of left hand (up-turned).
- Holding wrists together, bring right hand up and left hand down, resembling an alligator's mouth opening and closing.

Adding

- Place the horizontal right hand's index finger crossed at the center of the vertical left hand's index finger.
- This creates a "Plus", "Add", or "Adding" math sign, as shown.

Apples

- Extend your right hand's index finger and bend it in half at the knuckle.
- Gently twist knuckle into cheek as shown.
- This sign originated from the rosy cheeks children would get during cold winter months. Also referred to as "Apple Cheeks".

I see 2

Bears

- Extend all fingers on both hands.
- Bend all fingers slightly to resemble two claws.
- Cross arms over chest as shown.
- Pull clawed hands down slightly, showing that Bears have claws that could scratch you. Repeat.

Balancing

- Hold both flat hands out in front of you with palms down as shown.
- Move one hand up while moving the opposite hand down, showing the attempt at balancing something.
- Repeat.

Boats

- Hold both hands extended out, with palms up and close to you. Fingers should be tight together with both pinky fingers touching.
- Move both hands forward as one, in an up and down motion as if over bumpy waves. Repeat.

I see 2 🖖

Cows

- Roll both hands up into fists.
- Extend both thumbs and pinky fingers.
- Place the thumbs on either part of your forehead as shown.
- While keeping both thumbs in place, bend hands forward and back. Represents a Cow's horns.

Carrying

- Hold both hands with palms facing up.
- Move both hands sideways in an arch movement.
- Indicates moving something from one location to another.

Cookies

- Hold left palm up.
- With the right hand place it's five fingertips down on the left flat palm as shown.
- Move right hand in a back and forth movement.
- Indicates pressing out cookies with a cookie cutter.
  Note: Opposite hands may be used.

I see 2

Ducks

- Roll hand into a fist.
- Extend the index and middle finger together while also extending the thumb as shown.
- Bring top two fingers and bottom thumb together and apart like a Duck's bill opening and closing. Repeat.

Dressing

- Place both open hands, palms facing body, in front of you.
- Bring hands down, as shown, indicating the motion of clothing during dressing. Repeat.

Dolls

- Extend your index finger, bend it and hook it over the top of your nose.
- Gently slide your hooked index finger off your nose in a downward motion.
- Indicates that a doll can be lead by the nose.
- Repeat.

I see 2

Elephants

- Using either hand, hold hand flat with fingers extended, palm down, under your nose as shown.
- Slide your hand down in a curved downward motion.
- Indicates an Elephant's long trunk.

Eating

- Using either hand bring all five fingertips together as shown.
- Bring your hand towards your mouth, reversing to bring it away, and then towards your mouth again. Indicating that food goes in your mouth.
- This is also the sign for food, groceries.

Eggs

- Using both hands, extend both index and middle fingers on each hand. Hold both fingers together as shown.
- Tap each hand's two fingers together twice then pull hands apart.
- Indicates cracking an egg and pulling the shell apart.

I see 2

Frogs

- On either hand extend both your index and middle fingers.
- Hold these two fingers together.
- Place your hand near your throat.
- Move your two fingers up and down indicating the inflation and movement of a Frog's vocal sack.

Flinging

- Open both hands with fingers separated as shown.
- Move hands in an upward motion, in various directions, indicating that you are flinging objects randomly. (Example: leaves, confetti, balloons, flowers.)
- Repeat multiple times.

Flowers

- With either hand bring together five fingertips as shown.
- Place fingertips under one nostril and then under the other nostril.
- Indicates that you smell flowers.

I see 2

Giraffes

- Using either hand, cup hand in front of neck as shown.
- Move hand straight up indicating that the Giraffe has a long neck.

Getting

- Extend both arms with open hands.
- Pull arms back towards your body while making your open hands into closed hands.
- Indicates getting something.

Groceries

- Using either hand bring all five fingertips together as shown.
- Bring hand towards mouth, reverse away from mouth, then bring hand towards mouth again.
- Indicates that groceries are food that goes into your mouth. Note: Also the sign for food and eat.

I see 3

Hamsters

- Using either hand, extend index finger and middle finger as shown.
- Brush the two fingers against the tip of your nose.
- Indicates that a Hamster wiggles his nose.

Hugging

- Cross both arms to give yourself a hug.
- Facial expression will show whether it's a happy hug or a sad hug.
- Indicates how you hug someone or something.

Hats

- Take either hand and tap the top of your head.
- Indicates the area a hat is placed.

I see 4

Insects

- Using either hand, extend thumb, index finger, and middle finger.
- Place your thumb on your nose, as shown, while wiggling your middle and index fingers.
- Indicates that Insects have antennas.

Imagining

- Roll both hands into fists.
- Extend both thumbs and pinky fingers.
- Move both arms and hands in circles, as shown, on either side of your head.
- Indicates that your imagination is always working.

Ice Cream

- Using either hand, roll your hand up as you would to hold an ice cream cone.
- Move your hand in a circular motion as you would if licking an ice cream cone.
- Indicates you're licking the ice cream on a cone.

I see 1

Jaguar

- Using both hands, with open fingers, brush hands across your cheeks as shown indicating the Jaguar's whiskers.
- Then immediately change hand shapes holding index fingers and thumbs as shown.
- Move this hand shape randomly across your body to indicate the spots of the Jaguar.

Juggling

- Alternate both hands up and down as shown.
- Indicates the hand and arm movement of juggling.

Jellyfish

- Using either hand, stretch your chosen hand to the opposite side of your body as shown.
- Starting with an open hand, alternate opening and closing your hand while moving it forward in a wave motion.
- Indicates how a Jellyfish opens and closes to swim.

I see 3

Kittens

- Using both hands, bring the fingertips of the index fingers and thumbs together.
- Place hands on either side of the nose and pull hands away from nose.
- Indicates the whiskers on a Kitten.
- Note: This is also the sign for "Cat."

Kissing

- Using either hand pretend to kiss the palm of the chosen hand.
- Then take that same palm and place it on your cheek.
- Indicates a kiss being shared.

Kites

- Hold one hand flat with fingers pointing up.
- Take the index finger of the other hand and place it in the palm of the flat hand.
- Holding the two hands together as shown, wiggle both in an upward motion.
- Indicates a kite being flown with a string attached.

I see 3

Llamas

- Using either hand, bend your ring finger and middle finger down together to touch the tip of your thumb while holding your pointer finger and pinky finger up.
- In this position your hand will resemble the head of a Llama.
- Move your hand slightly left and right indicating that the Llama is alive.

Licking

- Using either hand, extend the pointer and middle fingers together as shown.
- Brush the two fingers up and down on the opposite palm simulating a tongue licking.

Lemons

- Using either hand, extend only the pointer finger and the thumb as shown making the letter "L" from the sign language alphabet.
- Place the thumb at the corner of your mouth as shown.
- While making a sour face, move your hand forward and back slightly. Indicates that lemons are sour.

I see 2

Monkeys

- Using both hands, pretend to scratch your body as shown.
- Indicates one of the actions of a Monkey.

Mopping

- Using both hands, pretend to hold the handle of a mop as shown.
- Push your hands forward and back indicating mopping a floor.

Milk

- Extend either arm away from your body as shown.
- Open and close your hand indicating milking a cow.

I see 3

Newts

- Since there is no sign for Newts, the word needs to be finger spelled.
- Sign the letters N-E-W-T-S, as shown above.
- Keep your hand in the same position and just change the hand shapes.

Needing

- Using either hand, extend your pointer finger while bending it at the knuckle as shown.
- Keeping your hand in this position, bring your hand down, bending it only at the wrist.
- Indicates you need something now.

Naps

- With eyes open and using either hand, place your open hand in front of your forehead as shown.
- While moving your hand down to your chin area, slowly close your eyes and close your fingers as shown.
- Indicates falling asleep. Also used as the sign for "Sleep."

I see 2 🖐️

Owls

- Using both hands, bring your hands to form two letter "O"s as in the sign language alphabet.
- Place the "O" hands in front of each eye as shown.
- Twist back and forth gently.
- Indicates the big eyes of an Owl.

Ordering

- Using both hands, extend your pointer finger, as shown.
- Move your fingers from your mouth to the location of the waiter or whoever will be taking your order.
- Indicates giving your order to a person.

Oranges

- Using either hand, make the shape of an "O," as in the sign language alphabet.
- Place your hand under your chin as shown.
- Open and tightly close your hand indicating squeezing the juice out of an orange.
- This sign is also used for the color "Orange."

I see 3

Puppies

- Using either hand, gently tap your flat hand against your leg and then snap (or pretend to snap) your fingers as shown.
- Indicates the action made when beckoning a Puppy or Dog.
- This is also the sign for "Dog."

Passing

- Using both hands, thumbs slightly extended and fingers curled in, keep your dominant hand stationary while your opposite hand passes by it, as shown.
- Indicates something being passed.

Popcorn

- Using both hands with palms up and fingers curled in, extend the pointer finger on one hand and quickly curl it back in.
- Repeat the same action with the other hand and continue by alternating between the two.
- Indicates popcorn popping.

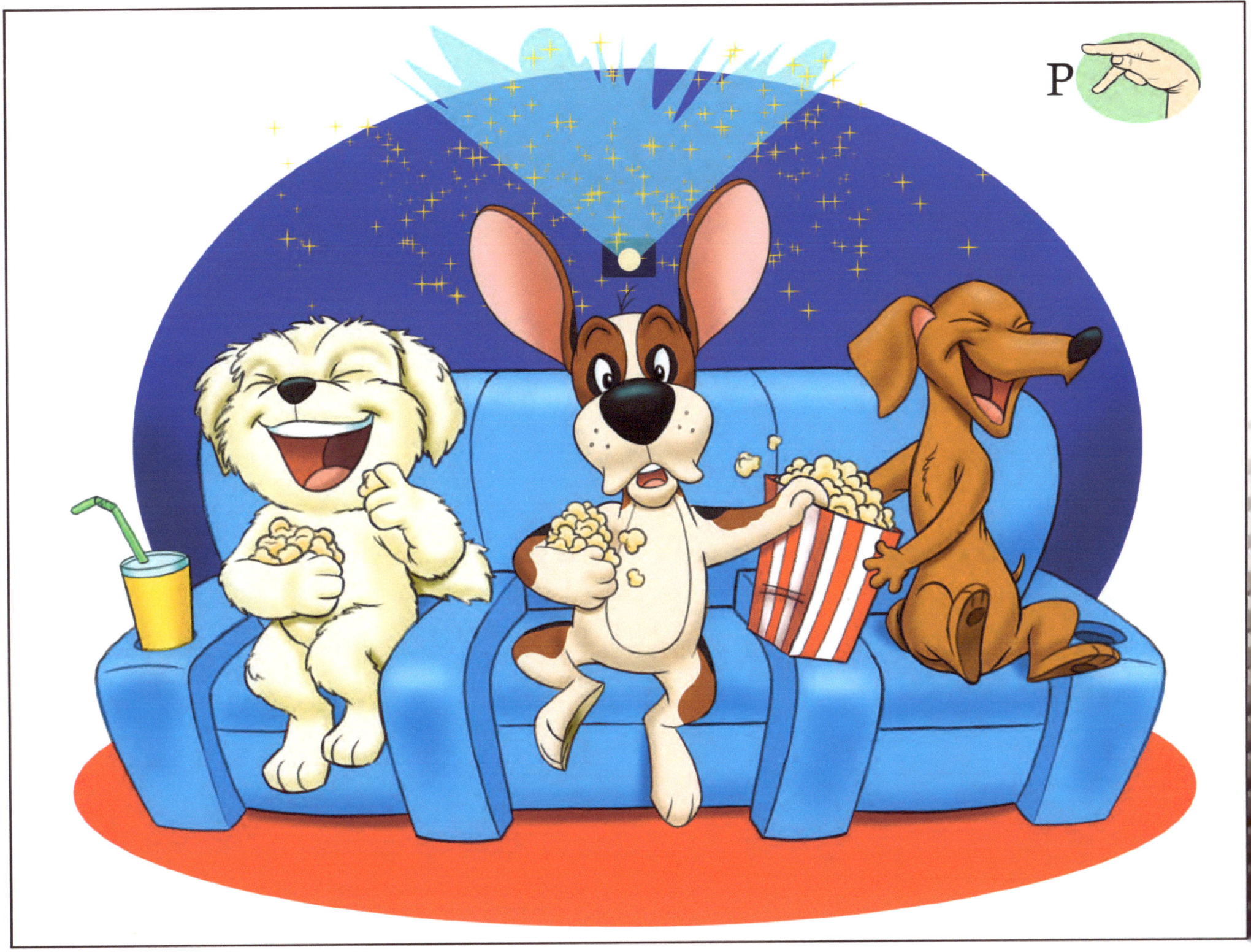

I see 2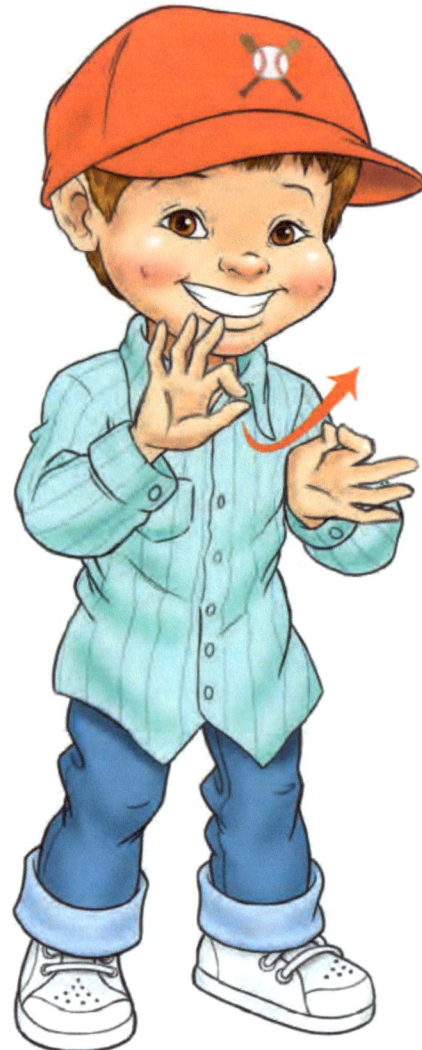

Quails

- Using either hand, extend your pointer finger.
- Place your hand toward the top of your forehead.
- Move your pointer finger slightly forward and back as shown.
- Depicts the single feather on top of the Quail's head.

Quietly

- Using both hands, place one flat hand with pointer finger close to lips similar to the "Ssssh" position.
- Place the opposite hand's pointer finger side against the bottom of the first hand's pinky finger as shown.
- Gently move each hand down and outward in the direction of each arrow above. Depicts quiet all around.

Quilting

- Using both hands, bring pointer finger and thumb together on each hand, as shown.
- With your dominant hand make a sewing motion toward the opposite hand.
- Depicts holding a needle and fabric while sewing.
- Also the sign for "Sew" or "Sewing."

I see 4

Rabbits

- Using both hands, extend both pointer and middle fingers together as shown.
- Cross arms, moving the extended fingers up and down depicting the ears of a Rabbit.

Racing

- Using both hands, extend thumbs while keeping fingers curled in.
- Keeping hands stationary, alternate tilting one thumb forward then back.
- Repeat the same action with the other hand.
- Alternate this movement between both hands, indicating a close race.

Rocks

- Using both hands, hold one hand with knuckles facing up as shown.
- Gently tap the opposite hand's knuckles on the bottom hand's knuckles.
- Depicts the hardness of a rock.

I see 2

Sharks

- Using either hand, bring your flat hand up to the front of your forehead.
- Depicts the fin of a Shark.

Slurping

- Using both hands, hold one hand as if holding a cup as shown.
- Hold the opposite hand's fingertips around the top of the cupped hand.
- Move top hand towards mouth while closing fingers.
- Depicts the drink going through the straw while slurping.

Smoothies

- Using both hands, extend pointer fingers.
- Rotate both fingertips around each other as shown.
- Depicts mixing the ingredients to make a smoothie.
- Note: Ingredients need to be signed or finger-spelled separately.

I see  1

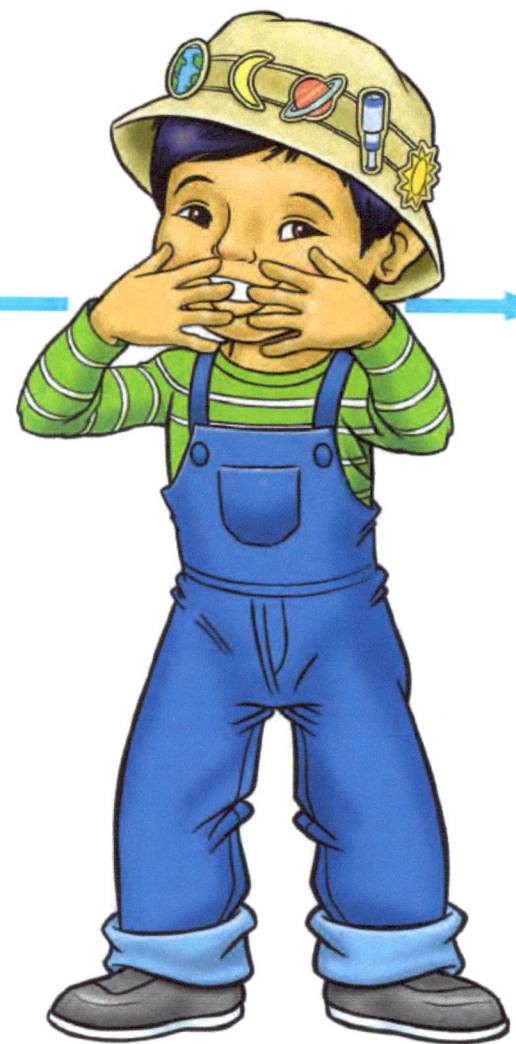

Tiger

- Using both hands, bring your extended fingers from under your nose outward as shown by the arrows above.
- Depicts the black stripes near the nose of the Tiger.

Texting

- Using both hands, place knuckles together as shown.
- Move thumbs randomly up and down.
- Depicts texting someone.

Thank You

- Using either hand, place flat hand in front of mouth as shown.
- Bring flat hand out and away from face.
- Depicts sending out a word of thanks.
- Also the sign for "Thanks, you're welcome," and "Gratitude."

I see 2

Unicorns

- Using either hand, cross your fingers as shown and hold your hand up on your forehead.
- Depicts the twisted horn of a Unicorn.

Under

- Using both hands, hold one hand out flat with palm facing down as shown.
- Hold the opposite hand over the flat hand with thumb extended up, then move the top hand under the flat hand.
- Depicts something under something.

Umbrellas

- Using both hands, hold one fist directly on top of your other fist, as shown.
- Move the top fist straight up.
- Depicts the opening action of an umbrella.

I see 2

Vultures

- First make the sign for "Bird" by extending your pointer finger and thumb and placing it in front of your mouth, moving the fingers up and down resembling a bird's beak.
- Second, extend all your fingers on your dominant hand, bending your middle finger downward as shown.
- On your other hand, extend and bend your pointer finger at the knuckle as shown.
- Circle your dominant hand's fingers around your other hand's bent pointer finger depicting the Vulture circling it's prey.

Vacuuming

- Using either hand, hold one hand out flat with palm up. Then hold your opposite hand, with fingers together, as shown with all fingertips touching the palm.
- Move the top hand from the wrist towards the direction of the arrow while puckering your lips and breathing in to make a vacuuming sound.
- Depicts the action of floors being vacuumed.

Vans

- Using both hands, hold hands in fists moving each hand in a semi-circle motion, as the arrows show.
- This depicts driving a van but it's also the sign for "Car" or "Vehicle."
- To specifically sign "VAN" finger-spell the letters. Refer to our alphabet page for the exact letter signs.

I see 2

Walruses

- Using both hands, roll each hand into a fist and place both fists below your cheeks.
- Bring your fists downward in a slight arch, as shown.
- Indicates the outline of a Walruses tusks.

Waking

- Using both hands, bring the index finger and thumb together in front of your eyes as shown.
- Keeping the hands in front of the eyes, open the thumb and index finger showing that the eyes open when you wake up.

Wizards

- Using one hand, place your hand on top of your head bringing the extended thumb and fingers into a point, as shown. Resembling the shape of a wizard's hat.

I see 3

Xiphosura

- Xiphosura are sometimes called Horseshoe Crabs.
- Using both hands, open and close hands as shown.
- Action resembles crab claws opening and closing.
- This is the sign for "Crab."
- The specific type of Crab, Xiphosura, must be finger-spelled. Please refer to our alphabet page.

X-Raying

- Using one hand, first bend the index finger half way to form the sign language letter "X" as shown.
- Then open the same hand extending all fingers.
- Place the open hand in front of the area or object to be X-rayed.
- For example, the illustration is showing the sign for chest X-ray.

Xylophones

- Using both hands, pretend to hold xylophone mallets.
- Move your hands up and down while moving your upper body from left to right.
- Indicates playing the music scales on a xylophone.

I see 2

Yaks

- Using one hand, form the sign language letters Y, A, K and S to finger-spell YAKS as shown above. (Also refer to our sign language alphabet page.)
- Note: Spoken words that do not have a designated sign are finger-spelled.

Yelling

- Using one hand, make a loose "C" shape and place it in front of your mouth.
- Bring this hand forward and upward from your mouth indicating the raising of your voice so it can be heard from far away.

Yogurt

- Using both hands form the sign language letter "Y" with one hand while forming the letter "C," held at waist level, with the other.
- Scoop the "Y" hand down to the "C" hand and back up to your mouth as shown.
- Indicates eating yogurt out of a cup.

I see 1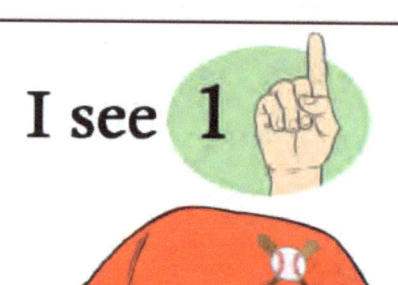

Zebra

- Using one hand, extend and separate all fingers.
- Place hand on opposite side of your body, as shown.
- Bend fingers to form a claw hand and gently drag your fingers across your body indicating the stripes on a Zebra.
- Repeat 2 times.

Zonked

- Note: Zonked is another word for Tired so the signs are the same.
- Using both hands, extend your fingers while holding them together in a bent position at the knuckles.
- Touch the tips of the fingers to either side of your chest with elbows held raised as shown.
- Keeping the tips of your fingers on your chest, suddenly drop your elbows and wrists while slouching your shoulders, showing that you are too tired to hold them up.

Zzzz

- Using one hand, extend your index finger and draw the letter "Z" as in the sign language alphabet, in the air.
- Repeat a number of times to represent snoring.

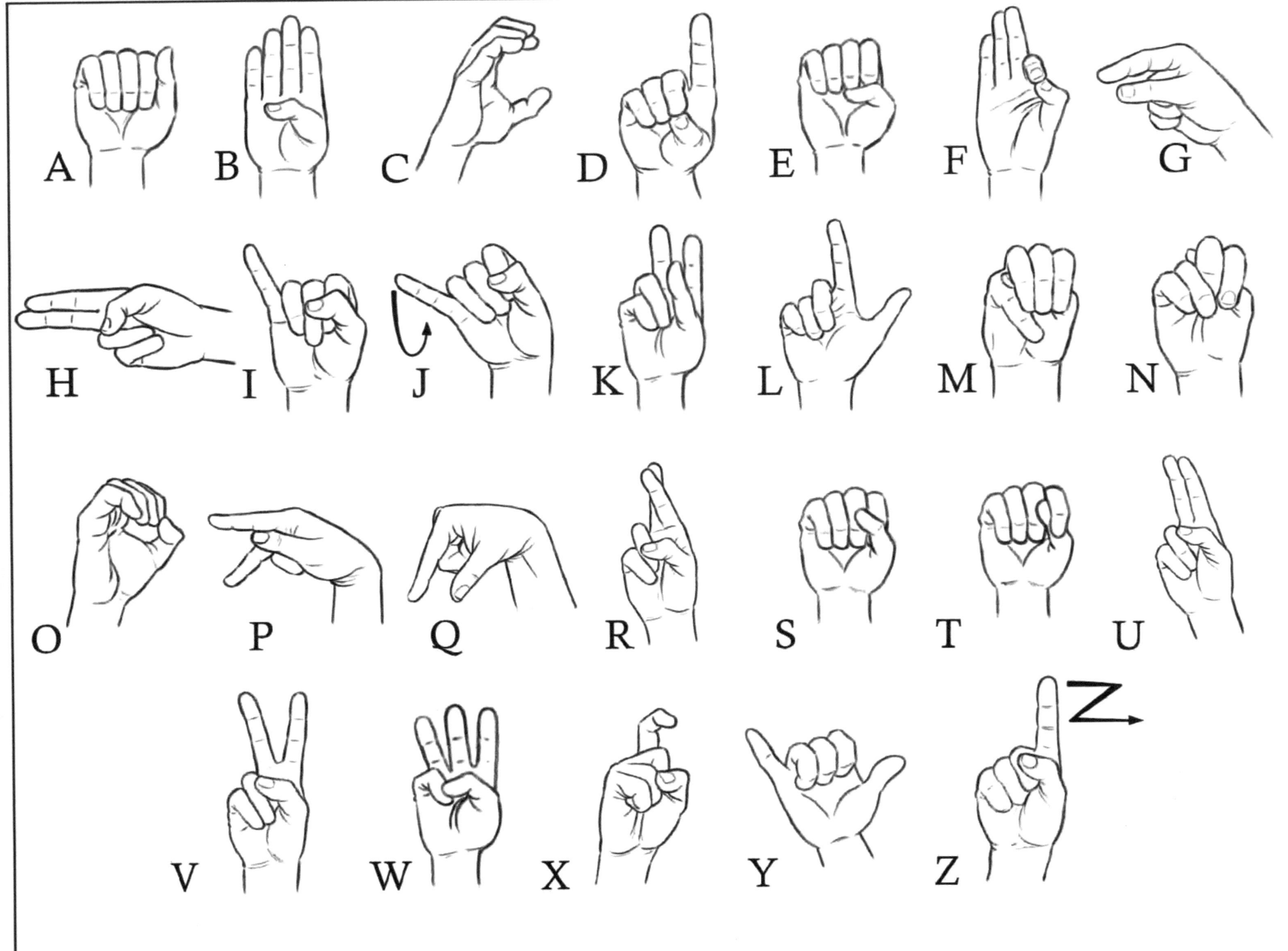

www.ingramcontent.com/pod-product-compliance
Lightning Source LLC
Chambersburg PA
CBHW041915230426

43673CB00016B/412